Eighty Eight

A poetic journey through
love, loss, choice, change, lies and truth.

Vicky Boulton

Dedicated to everyone who has made me feel.

CONTENTS

'I never regret anything. Because every little detail of your life is what made you into who you are in the end.'

— DREW BARRYMORE —

Innocence

innocence

Hope

Do you remember our moment of shared honesty?
As we were captivated and spurred on by apparitions
Of timeless images, hopes and dreams,
For a future which would fulfil our needs.
We were so eager for control, perhaps even power,
Nothing we thought, was beyond our reach.
The whole world was ours to take and break.

But we were too young and so naïve,
Mistakes happened and our paths widened,
To reveal the stark truth, the lie of reality.
Nothing is as it really seems to be,
No one is as trusting as you want to believe.
Our hopes and dreams were built on fantasies,
Easily crumbled, leaving nothing in their place.

It was too late as realisation dawned,
We knew then that we could take nothing more.
No longer could we be deceived by silent manipulations,
Which tragically resulted in little satisfaction.
Through the loss of innocence,
Acted on by an illusion called love,
I lost my ambitions as the hope in me died.

Forget reality

When I close my eyes, I see only you.
Brave and defiant; unafraid of what will happen.
I can feel you when you're not there.
I can taste you, even in my dreams.
For one night, we belonged together.
Reality forgotten, while passion ensued.
I knew then that it was over,
As quickly as it had begun.
Because I have neither the power, nor the strength
To keep you beside me forever.

Jealousy

Jealous of you?
You with the intellect and the beauty
And me positively plain beside you.
No, I am not jealous, because
I can have any man here,
Because I give my body
And my heart
Because that is all I've got to give.

Gone away

Even when you've gone from me,
To a world where satisfaction
Will quench your thirst for knowledge,
I'll remain here, silent in thought,
Remembering the poetry and intimacy,
Revelling in our past glory of youth
And never forgetting the bond between us.

You will discover more meanings
Than I could ever teach you.
And be accepted as easily as the beauty you possess.
But I'll remain here, quiet and alone
As memories creep into mind.
The flickering candle, the promising dreams
And our revelation of near perfection.

You will be happy in your Utopia,
And you will maybe forget about me,
As the desire for fulfilment drains your mind.
But I am always here, waiting for you.
I don't hold any claims on you,
The past has taken those away from me.
Making the friendship between us
A final conquest of injustice.

A definition

What is love
But a tangled web of suspended emotions?
An excuse for lies and venting of anger.
A black void in which we are trapped,
Pinned down with no form of escape.
Is this what love represents?
Is this what we yearn for?
To be owned, treated as a possession.
Bought with kind words and a smile.
Hurt and wounded by our naivety
And finally abandoned because we had feelings?
What madness is this love?
Like a drug it produces cravings of desire,
Jealousy, inferiority and then despair.

Repetition

I have been through this before.
I trusted you and made the mistake
Of thinking you were different.
But just like the rest,
You spoke the words I wanted to hear
And left when night became morning.
How could I have been so trusting
To fall for the same well-rehearsed lines
Again and again?

Modern fairy tale

'I love you,' I heard you whisper,
On a night that struggled with lust.
I wanted to reciprocate,
Say something that would make you feel wanted too.
But the words were held in a void.
It was what I had always believed in,
True love and happy endings like a fairy tale.
But when the moment arrived
I found myself unable to respond.
It was only afterwards I realised.
When the passion was removed.
The only thing remaining,
Were two naked souls hiding in shame
From the sharp light of reality.

First

Why should I have told you
That you were the first?
You were too busy to notice.
Too busy demonstrating your skill
In a well-practised performance.
I could well have not been there
As I was only an available body
For whom you probably did not even care.

What does it matter anymore?
You only took from me
What I was willing to give.
So, don't contemplate meanings
And demand my answers
To questions too difficult to ask.
You were the first
And believe me, it was nothing.

Everything is not enough

She had everything.
Many were envious of her fortunate ways.
Luck, happiness and good things followed her
Wherever she went.
She moved through life like a butterfly
Never standing still or reflecting
On what had gone before.
No one ever realised until it was too late,
That every butterfly needs a mate.

Change of heart

She did not love him anymore.
But unable to explain *why* to herself
Proved much harder than telling him.

Friendship

And when asked what I would remember most
About the times we spent together,
My mind conjured up so many images, words and feelings.

I remember the happy times of drunken idleness and the regrets
Which always followed the next day.
The frequent wild weekends when everything was done to excess.

But what of our sad moods, of which there were equally as many.
Tears, tantrums and feelings of loss,
And the recollections of great understanding and sincerity.

I remember the romantic times, repeating what we said endlessly
As if convincing ourselves it was real,
And was, after all, what we had always wanted to happen to us.

Our men, so different, so much fun, so wrong for both of us.
They remained always the cause of our problems,
And the reconcilers of our deep and everlasting friendship.

Experience

experience

Coffee and cigarettes

I love you more than the milk
In my coffee.
More than the last cigarette
Before I sleep.
More than the books
I always read.
More than the music
I listen to.
And even more than the person
Who slept there before you.

Look no further

When I'm alone, you always appear at my side.
And when I'm confused, you act as my guide.
When I'm sad, you understand all my fears,
And wait with me, until the unhappiness clears.

When I'm troubled, you slowly ease all my pain.
And when I'm angry, you show me there's no gain.
When I am silent, you know I like it that way
And you leave me alone, until there's something to say.

When I'm excited, you let me go slightly mad.
And when I'm laughing, you seem so glad.
When I'm happy, you share it with me.
And we're united together, the way it should be.

Paused in thought

'Nothing will ever be the same again,'
She whispered to herself.
Everything had changed,
Too dramatically to go back to
What had been,
And had then meant so much.
And as she groped for an explanation,
There was nothing there to be found.
Only the knowledge that
Nothing would ever be the same again.

Hurt

Crowds pressed against her,
Her body jerked back in revulsion.
To be touched so openly,
Handled so freely, disgusted her.
She could not join then in this tragic game,
As memories held her back, storming her brain.

She laughed at them,
Struggling against the hate she felt.
She kissed so meaningfully
With lust not love.
Mauled by strong hands, cradled in arms,
So harsh like her father's, would they hurt her too?

Embracing and crushing her,
She checked the repulsion in her throat.
Choking back tears of pain
She reached for the door.
The freedom which lay beyond it, a mere dream
But to be away from this room, became her only goal.

The explanation

If only things were different.
If only I weren't me.
I would try and make you realise
I want to make you see.

It's not that I'm so selfish.
It's not that I don't care.
It's because of him I'm leaving
Even though he won't be there.

I never meant to hurt you
That's not the way I play
But I've got nothing left to offer you
And there is nothing more to say.

Written word

Why am I writing so much, so late on in the evening?
It's as if I want to recapture every moment
Of our life together as it happens.
The love, the pain, the ecstasy and the despair.
Because when tomorrow comes, unrelenting and unbidden,
Today will become just another memory?

Clear thinking

Now he has gone.
How much clearer can I see
My life for what it was
And ultimately now should be.

Joker

You joke and say you love me
I say it too, but I'm not joking.
You laugh and flatter me
I sit and analyse my emotions.
You hold me close and touch me
I lie back and watch inwardly.
You smile as your lips meet mine
I remain quiet and respond gently.
You sigh as your body covers mine
I try to disappear, but I can't.
You move slowly capturing the final triumph
I move my head next to yours.
You whisper your thoughts so softly
I listen, but can I believe them?

Derelict

'I've nothing left to offer you,'
You said as you bent down
To retrieve your coat
On the way to the door.
'Nothing?' I repeated
And as the anger and frustration grew
I added, 'Did you ever?'

Next time

And sometimes do you wonder
If the next time it happens
Will signify the end of the line
Or the beginning of a circle?

Past love

Don't you ever on a night of trust and honesty
Lament on the loss of a past love,
Because it will only hurt you and others,
Destroying any future happiness, you both may seek.

The past is never to be revisited or explained.
It is to be quietly learnt from and used
As a building block for your future.
If you must indulge your mind in remembrance
Then wait until you are alone and your selfishness
Need not be witnessed by those you now love.

Truth and Lies

truth and lies

You and I

You and I.
Two different, two secretive
Powerful individuals
Who hurt because they could.

You and I.
Two similar, two deceptive
Wilful individuals
Who lied to save themselves.

You and I.
Two hasty, two manipulative
Selfish individuals
Who took one night of lust.

You and I.
Two lonely, two stubborn
Cruel individuals
Who tried to relive a dream.

You and I.
Two complicit, two reckless
Manipulative lovers
Who live with a guilty secret.

The lie that's me

When you look at me, what do you see?
Someone smiling confidently and oozing charm?
A person who will make something of their life
And is happy in their own skin?
That's what I don't understand.
Why I think the mirror must be wrong.
Because when I look, all I can see,
Is a big fat lie, pretending to be me.

Suitcase

You tried to explain
As you packed your suitcase.
You wanted to tell me everything
But I refused to listen.
So, I allowed you to remove
Your belongings from my life.
Knowing it was finally too late,
For explanations and justifications
Which can never change what happened.

Welcome to your truth

So, you didn't mean it.
Who cares?
You choose a different path
And carried the burden.
But it must have weighed heavily
Else why are you boxing
Your life into the car
That will take you from me?

So, you didn't love me.
Who cares?
You made me completely happy
And that's almost rare.
But it still wasn't enough
As the signs blinded you
Forcing a final decision
That did not include me.

So, your words were lies.
Who cares?
You needed an accomplice
And you choose me.
But why when truth came calling.
Loudly and without warning,
Did you choose to answer?
Hurriedly confess and then leave?

So, you left me alone.
Who cares?
You listened to your heart
And that's what matters.
But why in my newfound solitude,
Do I demand to know?
Whether love, truth or lies,
Were ever your real reasons?

The conversation

'What do you want?' she demanded
As the tears welled up inside her.
Accustomed to being an object of desire
She now feared for her rejection.
'You've hurt me,' he answered,
And with those three words he calmly
Confirmed her worst fears.
He knew the truth about her.
And the reason for the lies.

Gushing honesty

A dinner with friends ended most abruptly
When someone asked for my opinion,
On a trivial matter of little or no consequence,
In the scale of larger global issues.

However, a heady combination of bad day,
Week and month, forced my brain and mouth
To co-ordinate as if as one and before I could stop,
Words of pure honestly gushed forth.

To say their responses would make a great picture,
Would offend brilliant artists of unshaking repute.
But shock turned to horror as they realised my life was a lie,
Carefully constructed to appeal to those whose acceptance
I craved.

I left before they could say anything.
Before they could ask that dreaded question, 'Who are you?'
Before they realised, I was not
And had never been, one of them.

But now as I sit at another table,
With new acquaintances, eating yet another dinner,
I wonder how long I've got before
Pure honesty ruins yet another perfect performance.

Half-truths

If you ever see him again
And he asks how I am.
Say I am happy,
With someone special who completes my dreams.

If he asks anything more
And wants to know where I am.
Tell him I am travelling,
Somewhere exotic, exciting and far away from home.

It does not matter
That both you and I
Know that none of this is true.
But it is important to me that, he hears these half-truths
from you.

Not today

Hang on to your hopes
And I will fulfil them again.
Take my hand and let us walk away.
Steal my emotions and lose them
In the beautiful winter haze.
Throw away your memories,
Resurrect your dreams
And let us start again.

I want to fall in love
But not this afternoon.

Debt

This time last year I had everything I wanted.
Today I have everything I deserve.
When you greedily take more than you need.
The scales rebalance themselves, leaving you in debt.

Nobody

Fighting emotions behind a rigid mask
People never suspect.
But *you* did with your knowing smile.

You took me to a distant land
Where pretty words soothed me
And my ideals could not shield me.

You were so convincing.
I listened to your stories
And dreamed of our future together.

Washed along like a grain of sand
I followed you and believed everything
That you told me.

It was easier to accept than to doubt.
As to suspect would just make you the same
As the others who had been there before you.

Logic and reason

And the words are out of my mouth before I can
measure them.
Years of pent-up frustration and anger add weight to
their meaning.
As they hurtle through the air to your disbelieving ears.
For one moment I want to change the rules of our game.
For one moment I want you to be in my shoes.
Perhaps only then will you understand why I am the way I am
And why I must hurt you to protect myself.

After the pain of each accusation hits home.
And you reel from the agony that each syllable inflicts.
Take time to unwrap what's surrounding the words.
Because in those layers you will find logic and reason.
Because in those layers you will find the truth.
Perhaps only then will you appreciate the way I see things
And you can finally release the ropes that bind me.

Choice

choice

Fate or destiny

Is it fate or is it destiny,
When a choice is made
Or a decision is taken?

Is it chance or is it pre-ordained,
When a soul is saved
Or a life is wasted?

Is it kismet or is it luck,
When a lover is found
Or a heart is broken?

When all's said and done,
I now know the truth
Good and bad things happen, for no reason at all.

Why love?

Write us a story, they said.
That talks of love at its best.
An epic tale of eternal passion.
A bestseller that will beat the rest.

Paint us a picture, they said.
That shows the colour of a kiss.
An unbelievable tone and shade.
A richness that symbolises true bliss.

Sing us a song, they said.
That comes straight from the heart.
An absolute classic melody and tune.
A winner that will top the chart.

Show us the place, they said.
Where hope and happiness meet.
An idyllic and peaceful haven.
A sanctuary or place to retreat.

Tell us what happens, they said.
When someone shares your soul.
An enduring test of togetherness.
A relationship to make you whole.

Explain what transpires, they said.
When love starts to break down.
And you find yourself all alone.
Walking the streets of an empty town?

Tell us what ensues, they said.
When sorrow is all you can see.
And a life on your own seems suddenly.
The way it's going to be.

So, when the questions ceased.
I took the enquiring ones aside.
What do you really want to know,
And why do you think I have lied?

We want to know why, they said.
Why when you can choose.
Do you throw yourself at love,
As if you had nothing to lose?

Why when it's dangerous, they said.
And it can sometimes end in pain.
Do you trust your heart to another,
Not once but again and again?

Tell us the truth, they finally said,
Is love really worth the cost?
Because there are no guarantees,
And your future could simply be lost?

You think love is wrong, I said,
But in fact, it's just so real.
It's the reason for everything I do,
And behind what I think and feel.

55

It's the one thing in my life,
That makes me completely alive.
Love may be complicated and scary,
But without it I wouldn't survive.

Tell us, they said, one final time.
Tell us what we should do?
Surrender to its unbelievable power,
Or just wait for something new?

Just don't talk about it, I said,
Go out there and try to feel,
Discover the fuss for yourself
And know why love's the genuine deal.

A decisive mind

She with the decisions made years ago
Saw an incalculable reason to reassess her future.
A chance meeting, a subtle reminder of what
could have been,
Conflicting with the agreed path ahead of what must be.
Alone and frustrated at the finality of choice
She accepted where her future lay and tried to ignore
the warnings.

But decisions can be changed, they are never fixed.
And hunger can burn in a touch or a smile.
Hiding itself in kindness, it soon finds a way
To demolish your plans and release your soul
To finally be with that someone else who
Never featured in the master plan.

Escape

My only means of escaping
Those tormenting memories
And perverse tell-tale images,
Is by pretending it was all a bad dream.
We never met and the years we spent together never existed.

Meaningless waste

Do not talk to me about logic.
Do not stop me as I leave.
Do not ask me to explain.
This will always be an unanswerable event.
I want this to be an unanswerable event.

Do not carry on with loving me.
Do not pretend I was different.
Do not substitute another emotion.
This will always have a tragic end.
I want this to have a tragic end.

Do not watch as I decide my fate.
Do not ask for me to change it.
Do not wonder if it was real.
This will always be a meaningless waste.
I want this to be a meaningless waste.

Do not hate me as it begins.
Do not understand false meanings.
Do not tell me I am wrong.
This will always be my final farewell.
I want this to be my final farewell.

Do not hold me when I am dead.
Do not grieve for me at all.
Do not make me anything I'm not.
This will always be on my own terms.
I need this to be on my own terms.

Foolish ways

Who was the bigger fool?
Me for letting you into my life
And wanting to keep you there forever?
Or you for your lack of honesty
And your frequent disappearing acts
When I now know that you visited her?

Hang-ups

Don't think you can judge us.
Or believe that you know best.
Our reason for not having children,
Was a choice, not a failed test.
We love being a couple with
No dependents sapping our time.
And savings in our bank account,
To us that seems just fine.
We don't consider we are selfish,
And I know others can't believe,
How we fill our waking hours,
And what milestones we achieve.
We are quite simply happy,
Being two, not three or four.
So, if this presents a problem,
Please leave your hang-ups at the door.

Accusations

One accusation and then another.
Each word causes another scar
To appear across my perfect heart.
I loved you, but now you are ruining
My memories of our love,
In just a few short sentences.

Here then gone

Love, why do you pick the most unlikely times to appear
And the most difficult times to disappear?
And why when you move on, do you never leave,
Anything tangible or comforting in your place?

Different life

And if things had been different.
Would I still be here turning the pages
Of an empty heart?
Wondering why the past and its memories
Still have the power to hurt me?

Gone for a minute

If I scrunch my eyes shut tightly so the skin pulls taut,
I can no longer see you standing
In front of me, pleading for a change in my answer.

And if I can't see you, even though you are still there,
Perhaps last night and what happened
Could similarly disappear,
Leaving me free of you forever?

Games

games

Perpetration

With your ingenuity and accomplished wit
You've separated yourself from me.
Seeing you casting silhouettes on my ceiling
I want to reach out and enclose you,
Melt you into my arms, liquid sweet.
But you don't understand that.

I belong to yesterday when loved thrived,
When you told me that you cared.
I realise that I can never own you,
But now you sense nothing,
Clouding and hiding your sight
From my defects of loneliness.

I don't want gratitude,
As I try to search you for an opening.
A space into which I might escape
And where your silence will touch me
More than your demands can.
But it seems too impossible.

Treading on my emotions,
You drive me insane towards you.
Caught in your web of self-deceit
I become anyone you want,
A friend or perhaps just a lover.
How long can this continue?
How much further can you lead me,
Until you fall and fight against me
Seduced by your own errors?

Sweet to sour

I've grown tired of our little game, but it seems that you crave more.
Because as soon as I lost interest, you found someone else to adore.
I've heard she's very beautiful, everything a partner should be
But if she's so damned wonderful, why do you still want me?

Initially your communications were amusing,
But now they've lost their power.
As they slowly taint our love,
Changing memories from sweet to sour.

Here we go again

Same words, different tone.
Same husband, still alone.
Same routine, different day.
Same direction, just your way.

Same house, different view.
Same agenda, nothing new.
Same problem, different fight.
Same feelings, perhaps not quite?

New day, different end?
New attitude, hearts mend?
New outcome, same me?
New you, wait and see.

Dangerous game

I know that you want me, but just not as much
As the new wife whom you married in June.
But marriage doesn't seem to have stopped you
From seeking me out in a crowded room.

In fact, married life seems to suit you.
It provides the perfect cover for your lies.
And the nights that you spend without her
As we discover a passion that won't die.

I watch you together and smile to myself.
Pretending our friendship's just the same,
As it was when I first laid eyes on you
And before the start of our dangerous game.

We seem to work in a strange sort of way.
Opposites attract is clearly true.
But whatever happens I hope it's worth
Everything I've sacrificed for you.

No one my age comes without baggage
People who trust and depend on me.
I know that I've let everyone down
I'm just not the person I pretend to be.

I never set out to deceive those I love
If I could, I would try to be strong
Ignore you and your insatiable demands
Because deep down I know it is wrong.

But when this ends, as I know it must
I hope it's over quickly and without blame
Letting us get on with our lives apart
And a friendship that will never be the same.

So, when it's over, please just walk away,
Don't look back or revisit the past.
Because if you have a wife and I have a husband
Aren't we proof of why marriages don't last?

History

Why do you let me feel like this?
Alone and confused?
I have waited so long
That my heart, as well as my mind,
Is now closed to your protestations.

Where you left me

I'm not where you left me
In the layby in the pouring rain, when I got out of your car
And your harsh words followed me home.

I'm now somewhere different
Where hope thrives, ensuring the pain of my past
And its many mistakes remain hidden forever.

But on dark and stormy nights
With makeshift rivers flowing down empty streets,
I often wonder
If your soul was similarly wiped clean?

Night-time friends

At night in my bedsit
The ill-fitting curtains let in streetlight pollution
Casting shadows and shapes across the room.
Tatty furniture, lamp shades and heaps of clothing become
People, mythical creatures and animals.
In the semi-darkness, I give them names, identities
And concoct stories where they are my protectors,
Highly trained warriors, but more importantly my friends.
But this feeling of intimacy is all too fleeting,
When morning beckons with its need to illuminate
Everything in its path with stark brightness,
My new friends vanish quickly,
Perhaps better places to be?
Leaving me alone once more in my empty bedsit
With the ugly, brown curtains.

Leaving

You're leaving me
I can feel your behaviour changing,
Your tone altering,
As your mind constructs imaginary walls
For me to climb.

You're leaving me
I can feel the distance increasing,
Your routines slipping,
As your subconscious places obstacles
For me to avoid.

You're leaving me
I can feel your tolerance waning,
Your patience thinning,
As your list of wilful objections builds
For me to overcome.

You're leaving me
I can feel your indifference seeping,
Your mood shifting,
As your toxic plans gather pace
For me to comply.

You've decisively left me.
I feel almost completely numb.
Your final words,
Leave cuts across my heart
For someone else to mend.

Spectator sport

Lost in a world, in which I appear to play no part.
I seem to spectate, watch from the outside.
Unable to propel myself into the centre,
I feel like an outsider.
Forced to experience second hand
What seems so important to the influential.
I have neither the force of personality
Nor the courage to proceed any further.
I am caught on the exterior.
With only you beside me
To stop me
From giving up completely.

Us

Forceful in your dismissal, I beg for a reprisal,
A sign that you might need me, may even love me.
You hold your body from mine,
Watching my expression,
Sensing its meaning,
Yet never quite understanding.

And as you kiss me, for a brief second
I want to change the rules of our fabricated game.
Your touch evokes memories,
In which you play no part.
As your mind is closed
Whilst your heart is stilled.

I only require some words to stop myself from dreaming.
You have the power to break me completely,
Whilst I have only the power
To seduce and love you.
Although I'll never earn your respect,
I will make you pay for the loss of mine.

Kiss me again and shout.
Crush me to you and scream.
Your doubt has no force like my love.
My hand soothes your face, and you smile,
Only then to hide yourself from me.
Closed and barred.

I leave your room of self-deceit
Your tunnel of lies is beyond even me.
You watch me leave, helpless to follow.
Too proud to call me back.
Too disillusioned to make things right,
One final time, so late in the evening.

Karma

I wanted to watch you suffer.
I needed you to feel pain.
I hoped you'd think of others,
Instead of focusing on your gain.

I wanted to hear you apologise,
I needed you to see the cost,
I hoped you'd know the impact,
When everything was duly lost.

Because scales need to be balanced.
And you can't always just take.
Everything in life is not yours,
To use, wound or break.

Sometimes life chooses to hit reset.
Leaving it obvious for all to see.
In life there is always one winner,
And for once, I hope it's me.

Reality

reality

Past perfect

I am trying to recapture one moment
In all our time together
Which was perfect,
Perhaps too perfect.
You may not understand
Why I must do this?
But in that one moment
I recall no doubts or fears,
No pain or sadness,
Only a desire to be happy.
And at this stage in my life,
I desperately need to remember
That such a feeling can exist.

Strong enough

As the years pass and your body aches.
Not from passion, but from the pain of living.
My advice to you all is to not be alone,
Because there's merit in sharing and giving.

But the best tip I heard was from a cheesy sitcom.
Where an old woman talked at length to her son.
Initially bewildered by the long list she mentioned,
He soon realised the way things needed to be done.

Find someone who'll listen to the good and the bad.
And never judge you for what you have said.
Find someone who'll sit with you day after day.
And never interrupt the thoughts in your head.

Find someone who'll love you come hell or high water.
And never wish for a different time or place.
Find someone who'll share your complex feelings,
And never knowingly invade your personal space.

Find someone who brings out the best of you.
And never once looks at their watch or leaves.
Find someone who'll be there come what may.
And never crumble as your heart openly grieves.

You may wonder where you'll find someone,
Who will do all these things just for you?
I think you'll find you already know them.
And that your lives are bound tightly like glue.

Because when I wanted that special person
I didn't have to look too far.
Although keeping his usual low profile,
My husband is always my star.

They offered me the world

They offered me a house, a car and a job
So perfect in nature that I would be secure forever.
But I realised that they would be empty
Without you there to share them.

They offered me a ticket, a passport
To the destination of my choice.
But I realised that the only place
I ever wanted to be was next to you.

They offered me money, so much that
I would never want for anything again.
But I realised that I could never buy
Either you or your love.

They offered me my health, a guarantee
That I would outlive most other people.
But I realised that if you weren't beside me
Life would not be worth living.

They offered me happiness, a dreamy existence
So beautiful and serene in its entirety.
But I realised that if you weren't there
I would lose my reason to function.

They offered me love, the freedom
To choose the perfect partner for life.
But I realised that the decision
Had effectively already been made.

And as a final gesture, they offered me the world
With everything in it and begged me to take it
But I knew that if the world existed without you
There would be no place in it for me.

And they gaze at me even now
Still struggling to comprehend my adamant refusals.
At the fact that I gave up everything so easily
Because of my love for you.

Ambition

It's funny how those teenage dreams of,
Changing the world.
Making a difference.
And setting hearts alight.
Now come down to,
Baking the perfect cake.
Growing beautiful yellow roses.
And medicating a poorly dog.
So, did I settle?
Or were my ambitions clipped
To match my modest abilities?

What's marriage about?

Your job prospects are not that important.
Nor the riches you have to your name.
It's whether when plans start to falter,
You work together without apportioning blame.

Your exclusive house is not really the issue.
Nor the cost of your new sports car.
It's whether when dreams start changing,
You can both reach for the brightest star.

Frequent foreign holidays are not the priority.
Nor the vast knowledge that you gain.
It's whether when you lose something special,
You join as if as one to fight the pain.

Expensive items are not the objective.
Nor the designer clothes you wear.
It's whether when hopes are dashed,
You can show how much you care.

Wealth and success are not the focus.
Nor the dreams that make you whole.
It's whether when life shows no mercy,
You come together to save your soul.

And it's not about the stories you tell.
Nor the name dropping you like to do.
It's whether when things hit the fan,
One plus one really does make two.

Because regardless of possessions and wealth.
Love's worth is not easy to count.
Because when you have a marriage,
Its value is not something to doubt.

The decorator

Until today I never really thought of myself as a decorator.
But as I ingeniously paper over the cracks
In our floundering relationship,
Ensuring that blame, resentment and indifference
Are all carefully concealed from family and friends
And those who witnessed our vows,
I begin to wonder what else I could turn my hand to?

Politics? I'm already an experienced and believable liar.
Accountancy? I'm well practised at adding and
subtracting lies.
Engineering? I can confidently build bridges and construct
valid excuses.
Medicine? I can deliver a negative prognosis
with a polite smile.
Author? I can craft fictional stories to explain our situation.

Or should I simply become a realist and finally face up
to the truth of our self-made disaster and leave?

Will you?

When you have everything but it's not enough
And the hole is too big to ignore.
Will you try something new and incredibly brave
Or stay safe and continue as before?

When you lose someone special who cannot be replaced
And the world shrinks to a big fat lie.
Will you look for new excitement in places unknown?
Or stay safe and never question why?

When you forget why you do the things that you do
And you wonder what's really at stake.
Will you remind yourself of the beauty of choice?
Or stay safe and watch everything break?

When your outlook changes from blue to grey
And you struggle to save your own heart.
Will you design your own path to happiness?
Or stay safe and ignore a new start?

When your reasons for being are slightly blurred
And you believe all your friends have left.
Will you stand up and shout for attention?
Or stay safe and feel utterly bereft?

When your purpose for living escapes you
And you exhale your very last breath.
I will be there beside you forever,
Keeping you safe, not in life, but in death.

If you loved me

If you loved me
You wouldn't hurt me.
If you loved me
You wouldn't cheat on me.
If you loved me
You wouldn't blame me.
If you loved me
You wouldn't lie to me.
If I loved you
I wouldn't leave you.

…Turns out I don't love you.

Great expectations

You do not want my help
Or the solutions that I find.
You do not want information
That may help to change your mind.

You do not want results
Or things to fare very well.
You do not want facts
That may make your life less hell.

You only want some free ears
To mouth off without care.
Someone to endlessly listen
Someone who's always there.

But if I get ahead of myself
Suggest a path not previously taken.
You shut me down quickly
And encourage my senses to waken.

So today I made a choice
One you forced me to do.
When it comes to preservation
I choose me first and not you.

The harder they fall

The pedestal I built was unfeasibly wide
And perhaps a shade too high.
I put people on it whom I trusted, loved
And for whom I'd ultimately die.
But in the end it wasn't its size or shape
That bothered me one bit.
It was the fact I once thought enough of you
To put you on top of it.

Complications

I used you that night.
Enclosed you in complications.
But you were different.
You loved me.
You listened to me.
Even when everyone else
Saw fault in my perfect lies.

I took you for granted.
Let you believe something.
But you were trusting.
I must go.
I won't come back.
So, it's time you realised
This does not have a happy ending.

Endings

endings

Final release

Silently waiting for a release,
An excuse not to stay around anymore.
Your words of initial innocence are
Now songs of experience.

But I am happy as you walk away.
That I was the one to change you
To mould, shape and prepare you to face
Someone else. Someone new.

But I am sad as you walk away
As you were the one to change me,
The one who made me realise
That after you…there would be no one else.

Ready?

When they took you away, I was relieved.
Relieved by a decision I had been helped to make.
I was free of everything once again,
As emotion and guilt eased slowly away.
But when sentiment left, pain happily took hold.
Feeding on insecurities, it established a home.
Whenever I failed, it punished me with memories
Sepia enclosed, confused but quietly clawing.
I clung to the past and wished for change
But change when summoned isn't always kind.
So, when your call came, I was waiting,
But you were not ready or even prepared,
As me and my neediness quickly suffocated you
Extinguishing any happy ending dreams, you had carried,
And deftly grinding your imaginings into dust.
The more I shared, the quicker you ran.
Until the distance between us
Was further than it had ever been.
Pain held up its hands to claim victory.
As your angry words bulls-eyed their target
And our fragile relationship crumbled before my eyes.
So, here I am alone again.
Forced to finally close the lid,
On my thirty-year-old box of dreams.

The break

You just don't realise how difficult it has been
Trying to forget that you exist.
Attempting to block out those tell-tale images of you and me.
Hoping that I'll never have to see you again.
Yet wishing that you had never left.

What does it matter anymore how I feel?
You knew I loved you, more than you loved me.
But when you left, with a goodbye
Which I denied having heard.
I knew then that I needed the courage,
To forget you and mend my broken heart.

Life's disappointments

Would you come back to me one day
If life had disappointed you
And yet another love had failed?

Would you sit me down and relate
Everything which had befallen you
Since we last met?

Would you want my advice and counsel
As you unburden your secrets
Desires and ambitions?

Would you do any of this,
Knowing how fiercely I once tried
To stop you from leaving me?

When love is one sided

'Promise you'll not contact me again?
Say you won't phone, write or try to find me?
Let me go quietly, release me so I can be finally free.'
She asks, eager to be gone.

He is silent for a moment, weighing up the enormity of
what she is asking.
Reluctant to agree to her demands,
But knowing there is little choice,
He asks her one final question.

'Will you always remember me
and all of the times that we've shared?'

She turns to him smiling, with eyes brimming with tears.
And says: 'I'll never forget you, not in a million years.'

No longer

Not everything is what it seems.
Nightmares conjured instead of dreams.
With the greatest lies often hidden,
Truth only appears when it is bidden.
Sometimes words can't convey what's real.
You need to watch closer for the ultimate deal.
As actions seek to lay bare the fact.
That my life is now just one big act.

His existence no longer makes me ache.
His absence does not make me break.
His look no longer makes me smile.
His love does not sustain every mile.
His need no longer matches my own.
His touch does not make me moan.
His words do not bring any relief.
His presence just signals endless grief.

Watch as I move from his embrace,
Eyes pleading openly to give me space.
Instead of passion there is only pain.
Reliving past failures again and again.
But as anger burns into something new.
Removing memories that once were true.
I want to be away from this childish game.
Finally free of him and any chance of blame.

So, as I make the final move to go.
Strong and focused with no fear on show.
I watch his face start to fade from sight.
As I journey towards the brightest light.
My spirit rallies as I struggle to be free.
Taking me closer to finding the new me.
No longer afraid of going it alone.
Just eager for my heart to be welcomed home.

Love without boundaries

The thrill and obsession of wanting you,
Destroyed ideals that once were true.
You took my heart and watched it bleed,
As I embraced lust and ached with need.

With desire and love slowly merging as one,
It was easy to forget why this was so wrong.
Vows and promises were simple to dismiss,
When I felt myself yield to your passionate kiss.

We became a game that was fun to play.
I believed in us and hoped we'd stay
A secret forever, hidden from view.
But discovery was swift once someone knew.

It ended horribly, as I knew it must,
Three relationships broken by a lack of trust.
Hate and accusations scar my foolish heart
As the pain of true loss rips me apart.

And on nights alone when I yearn to be free,
I remember my mother's words to me.
'Like lovers with hearts brimming with guilt,
Wildflowers once picked, will quickly wilt.'

Why scenario

That girl used to be me
Happy, fearless but mostly carefree.
Her life used to be my life
Fun filled and satisfying without any strife.
Her home used to be my home
Before I was set free to roam.
Her place used to be the place
Where I met love face to face.
Her heart used to be my heart
Until it was cruelly ripped apart.
Her vice used to be my vice
Before someone rolled the dice.
Her pride used to be my pride
Until good nature went for a ride.
Her dream used to be my dream
But things are never what they seem.

Twenty years later and it's painful to see,
Characteristics disappear that were once part of me.
But worse than the fact that it seems so unfair,
Is what it comes down to is...I don't really care.

Dead love

On the morning you walked out of my life,
You left no explanation, no words or gestures
To be interpreted either rightly or wrongly.
There was no fight, no argument and no blame
To be shared equally between the two of us.
So, with nothing to analyse and no reason for us to be apart,
I realised that I must bury our dead love alone.

Lost

I have lost you and I am lost.

News delivered by a foolish colleague robs me of sense
And I watch myself plunge.
Freely, faster and further than ever before.

Her shock at my reaction reminds me just how complicated
we have become.
And I wonder if my fall from grace will be reported back
to those who think they know more.

She leaves and realisation breaks.
Knowing I cannot touch or kiss you one final time.
Never sleep or wake with you by my side.
Never watch your brilliant face as it turns to mine.
All sound the final drumbeat on our guilt-laden half-life

I cannot grieve; I do not deserve that simple right
I cannot lay claim to your love or expose our truth.
I am doomed to stand on the touchline,
watching others feel your loss,
Whilst trying not to remember how it felt to be loved by you.

In a contest between wife and lover,
There is only ever one winner.

Perhaps that's as it should be – the final justice
for taking something that was never really yours.

Where does love go?

Where does love go when we say we no longer care?
Where do feelings hide when we wave a final goodbye?
Where does passion live when it loses its brilliant spark?
Where did you run to when we became you and me?

Gone

Now you're gone.
I realise how I failed to keep you safe.
Innocent with the belief that we had forever,
I grew careless, forgetting my need to protect you.
So, when it happened.
So quickly and so terribly.
My pain and grief became riddled with guilt.

Now you're gone.
I know I should have done more.
Cherished every moment we shared.
Refrained from wishing for something different.
And now it's over.
And nothing can fill the space.
My life is fractured into sharp memories that hurt.

Now you're gone.
I go through the motions of existing.
Wondering why we never talk about you.
Why your death has become socially awkward.
I don't want sympathy.
I don't need soothing words.
To sum up the brief happiness that we shared.

Now you're gone.
I see things much clearer than before.
Mystified by answers to the question "why".

I feel locked in by my decisions and actions.
I can't move on.
I can't forget how it feels,
When I remember the promises that won't be kept.

Now you're gone.
I must remove items from my sight.
Things that cause me to suddenly falter.
Gasp for breath, as I process the future.
Today is tough.
Today is different from yesterday.
As I modify my behaviours to fit with what's expected.

So, as I wipe every trace of you from my life.
Eradicating toys, smells and things to a hidden place.
I close my eyes and conjure up your face
Your presence and the joy you brought.
Hoping one day, we will meet again
And you will not judge me for what I did.

Well lived

I'm not scared of dying.
I'm afraid of not living.
Of having regrets, plans unfulfilled and ideas not actioned.

I fear missing the sunrise, the first snowdrop
The crunch of footsteps on newly laid snow.
And the rich colours of autumn.

I want one more view of an aquamarine sea.
A final taste of the sourness of lime.
One last smell of freshly cut grass.

Precious seconds to witness the kindness of strangers.
The feel of sand between my toes.
And the sound of waves crashing on the shore.

Only then, will my life be complete.
Only then, will I be ready to look into your eyes,
Whisper goodbye and give thanks for a life well lived.

Vicky Boulton grew up in North Yorkshire. Fascinated by words, she started writing poetry aged 10 and has no intention of stopping any time soon.

Eighty Eight, is Vicky's first anthology.

Vicky lives in rural Northamptonshire with her husband and several dogs.